Collective Nouns Abound!

Julia Lynne Cothran

Illustrated by Leigh Ellen Stewart

Archway Publishing books may be ordered through booksellers or by contacting:

Archway Publishing
1663 Liberty Drive
Bloomington, IN 47403
www.archwaypublishing.com
844-669-3957

Illustrations by Leigh Ellen Stewart

ISBN: 978-1-6657-4657-1 (sc)
ISBN: 978-1-6657-4658-8 (e)

Library of Congress Control Number: 2023912352

Print information available on the last page.

Archway Publishing rev. date: 7/14/2023

Dedication

During the 15th Century, a St. Alban's nun near Hertfordshire, England is credited with inventing collective nouns. Julia Berners wrote a book titled **Hawking, Hunting, and Blasing Arms** a reprint of the 1486 text **The Book of St. Albans** which later added a chapter on fishing. Berners was most likely born into nobility, received an education, and had a love for field sports. She is also noted as being the first author to chronicle the strategies of angling.

Acknowledgements

Alan Cothran who is guiding me from above.

To my parents and step-parents Jane and Charles Jackson and Roy and Diana Cothran

To illustrator extraordinaire Leigh Ellen Stewart and her husband, Mark and grandson, Lawson, for valuable guidance, support, and friendship.

To my aunt Judy Anne Funderburg for introducing me to Julia Berners.

Special acknowledgement to my late aunt Sara Cothran. She was always interested in what I was doing.

To my aunts: Janie Cothran, Joey Cothran, Barbara Cothran, Mary Lee Cothran Clark, Kem Cothran, and Jimmie Cothran

To the following people for inspiration, assistance, and constant interest:

Kristin Jarzab, Lesley Cothran Emerson, Natalie Drury, Makenzie Drury Griffin, Tracy Beach Martin, Gayle Edwards, Melissa Paschall Bogard, Ange Paulter Dierks, Christy McCallon, Ella Chambers, Maddox Inman, Hendrix Inman, Constance Alexander, and Judy Shoffner.

And finally, to my dog Max who endured endless hours of listening to me.

In this book
I think you will find

that collective nouns
are one-of-a-kind.

Each collective noun
represents two or more,

and on these pages
you'll find them galore.

Now, start at the beginning
and you'll learn each phrase.

These collective nouns
go on for days!

Whether in the air or on the ground,
Collective Nouns Abound!

An **ambush** of tigers

An array of hedgehogs

An **ascension** of larks

And an army of frogs

A caravan of camels

A congress of baboons

A **thunder** of hippos

And a mask of racoons

A turn of turtles
A wake of buzzards

An earth of foxes
And a sord of mallards

A host of sparrows
A prickle of porcupines

A **wisdom** of owls
Basking in the sunshine

All of these words
are distinctive by nature.
It's a unique way
to **group** each creature.

A fever of stingrays
A marvel of unicorns

A team of horses
And flies are a **swarm**

A company of parrots
A congregation of crocodiles

A cornucopia **of slugs**
And a watch of nightingales

A loft of pigeons
A leap of leopards

A party **of** jays
And a **fall** of woodpeckers

A trip of goats
A passel of pigs

A **lodge** of beavers
With some wearing wigs

Rather than "bunch" or "many"
these specific words will do:

a leap, a mask, an army, a charm
are just some terms to name a few.

A **rake** of mules
A clash of bucks

A bed of eels
And a raft of ducks

A **clew** of worms
A cloud of gnats

A **charm** of falcons
And a **colony** of bats

A **bouquet** of pheasants
A ballet of swans

A barrel of monkeys
And a leash of fawns

KALEIDOSCOPE CLUTTER LITTER MISCHIEF CLOUD CHARM COLONY CLEW TRIP PASSEL RAFT #ALL CORNUCOPIA WATCH KATIE CONGREGATION TEAM SWARM LOFT PARTY FEVER COMPANY RAKE BED LEAP CLASH BALLET LEASH BARREL

Some terms are the same
to label each creature.
But, all of the nouns
are collective in nature.

A down of hares
A down of sheep
A down of rabbits
All snoring as they sleep

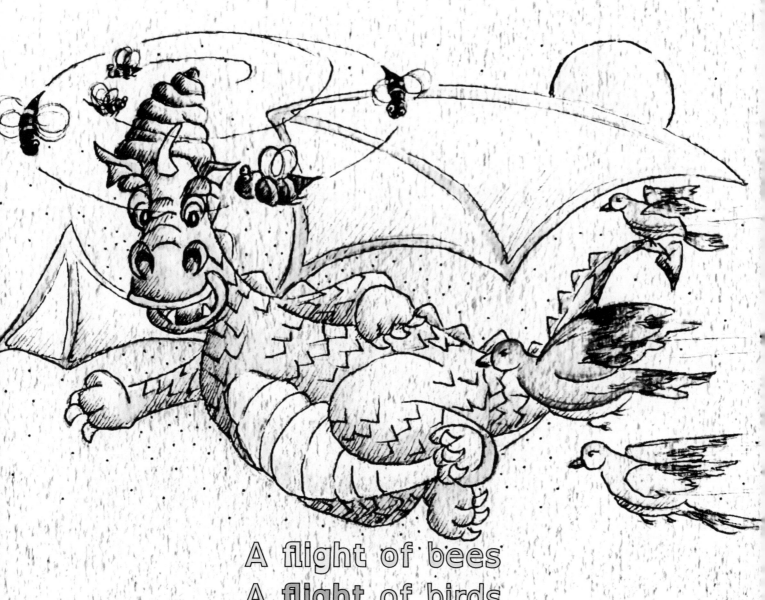

A flight of bees
A flight of birds
A flight of dragons
All use the SAME word

A **mob** of meerkats
A **mob** of kangaroos
A **mob** of wallabies
And a **mob** of emus

A **herd** of cattle
A herd of seahorses
A **herd** of seals
And ditto for walruses

So, when you think
you have it together,

use these names for animals
covered by hair, scales, fur, and feathers.

About the Author

Lynne retired from the Kentucky Public School System after teaching language arts for twenty-eight years at the elementary and middle school levels. She holds a master's in elementary education from Murray State University and a master's in principalship and supervision from Indiana State University.

Her first book is titled *Does a Gaggle of Geese Giggle?*. Her second book is *Collective Nouns Abound!* She uses humor and rhyme to inform and entertain readers. She calls it "unintentional learning." The reader absorbs the information through vividly illustrated watercolor paintings and verse.

Her joys in life are working with children and animals. She has a dog, Max, and a cat, Fendi.

About the Illustrator

Leigh Ellen Stewart is an eclectic artist producing works of art with a wide range of subject matter, techniques and media. Spiritually blessed and inspired by family/friends, Leigh was first introduced to visual art at an early age pursuing a more formal education with degrees in Art Education from Western Kentucky University. Leigh has retired from a rewarding 33 year professional career in the public school system and from a small, family owned business that specialized in the advancement and works of local and regional artisans. Currently, Leigh focuses on creative time with family and works from home.

Printed in the United States
by Baker & Taylor Publisher Services